# FEATURE: RECONSTRUCTION

## Shezad Dawood

# FEATURE: RECONSTRUCTION

## Shezad Dawood

Book Works
2008

# FEATURE: RECONSTRUCTION — A SYNOPSIS

Gerrie van Noord

What do Chief Crazy Horse, Krishna, a Valkyrie, a bunch of Zombies and some fetish boys have in common with a donkey and an albino snake? Nothing, when we rely on our conventional way of remembering stories and histories, and our inclination to keep different cultural contexts and frames of reference apart. The film *Feature* (that started as a figment of Shezad Dawood's imagination) however, seems to play havoc with the unwritten rules that determine these boundaries between cultures and peoples, and distinctions between fact and fiction.

*Feature* clearly isn't a conventional film based on the format of traditional Westerns. David Medalla labels it a 'Zombie Western' and credits artist, director and actor Shezad Dawood with creating an entirely new genre. Mixing and mingling, linking entirely different historical moments with mythology, and intertwining generally shared with intimately personal histories are what distinguish *Feature*.

Although American Westerns have a history of being shot elsewhere (the Spaghetti Western no doubt their most well-known sub-genre), with locating the action in the undeniably English Cambridgeshire countryside, the film could have been called *Feature: Relocation*. But the displacement doesn't stop there: large, clearly fake, painted cacti (produced by a scene painters' studio in Karachi) litter the landscape.

It could also have been called *Feature: Reconsidered*. By titling it simply *Feature* though, the emphasis shifts away from Western and Zombie film references, to notions of cinematic time and process with winks and nods to Buster Keaton and Samuel Beckett. Having said that, *Feature: Recast*, *Feature: Reshot* or *Feature: Reimagined* could just as easily have been title contenders.

The film's cast equally turns our expectations upside down and inside out. Traditional masculine characters are paired with half and whole deities and more profane characters. Starring General Custer, Sitting Bull (artist Jimmie Durham), Crazy Horse (artist David Medalla), the Sheriff (artist Doug Fishbone), some fetish Bartenders and Billy de Krishna (Shezad Dawood) as well as Hetna the Valkyrie (opera singer Hetna Regitze Bruun) and many more, including the Lonesome Cowboys, the Fairhaven Singers, The Outlaws and C4, the Cambridge Chinese Community Centre Football team.

The plot develops along similarly unexpected lines: Crazy Horse and Krishna share a pipe and while in a mystical trance foresee the coming of Ragnarök (the end of the world, according to Norse mythology). Amid one of the war scenes, Crazy Horse gives up his life (his horse and his head-dress) for General Custer. Dead cowboys stir from the battlefields and the Zombies head into town for a drink, killing the Sheriff on the way to the bar. Krishna comes back to life and encounters a Valkyrie who leads a group of Zombies while singing a section of Wagner's *Ring Cycle*. Krishna kills the Zombies in a blaze of gunfire and then comes face to face with his ancient foe. They kiss, and cultural oppositions are rendered null and void. The End.

In line with the 'mix it up and start again' ethos of the film, this book isn't a straightforward 'the making of' or simple documentation of the process. No official stills here. Instead a wide range of shots capturing the action on both sides of the camera, taken by actors and volunteers, professionals and amateurs. An open casting weekend at Wysing Arts in Cambridgeshire in September 2007 started this blurring of boundaries and roles between those hired and those coming along for fun.

No official, lengthy script here either. Instead, a series of sketches that formed the basis of improvisations for all the actors and extras. No analytical essays, but small footnotes with factual information relating to the various cultural frames of reference that collide in the film's epic story. Snippets of communication between the producer, assistant producer, director, director of photography, costume maker, make-up artist and owners of donkeys, horses and snakes and many assistants shed a light on the unusual production process of this multi-layered project. The written and visual contributions by Jimmie Durham, Doug Fishbone, David Medalla and Sebastian Roach, add yet more layers to the reconstruction of what happened on and off set, merging the fictional and real-life characters. In the end *Feature: Reconstruction* shows us that events, stories, histories and mythologies live on in our common memories, but can remain open for our own regular re-interpretation.

# SHEZAD DAWOOD FEATURE

**FREE DROP IN EVENT**

Try out for a part in a 'Western' film Wysing Arts Centre has commissioned from artist Shezad Dawood. On the 15 and 16 September, Wysing's site will be transformed into a Western film-set complete with super-sized painted backdrops, mineshafts, an 'Indian settlement' and Wagons.

Come along and try-out for the production and if you have your own Western clothes, come along in costume.

Casting sessions are aimed at adults, although the event is suitable for all ages with FREE drop in children's workshops. Dress up and bring a picnic!

Saturday 15 September 2–5pm
Sunday 16 September 2–5pm

# W

**WYSING ARTS CENTRE** Fox Road, Bourn, CB23 2TX
T +44 (0)1954 718 881  www.wysingartscentre.org
Join our E-Bulletin at info@wysingartscentre.org

Children must be accompanied at all times. Please note the event takes place across some uneven ground.

Jimmie Durham as The Narrator

# SCENE 01:
# OUTLAWS

POKER GAME
(WITH POSSIBLE
FIGHT?)

**CAPTAIN SIR RICHARD FRANCIS BURTON**
(19 March 1821 – 20 October 1890) was
an English explorer, translator, writer,
soldier, orientalist, ethnologist, linguist,
poet, hypnotist, fencer and diplomat.
Burton's best-known achievements include
travelling in disguise to Mecca, making an
unexpurgated translation of *The Book of
One Thousand Nights and A Night* and the
*Kama Sutra.*

**CRAZY HORSE** (ca. 1842 – 5 September 1877)
was a respected war leader of the Lakota,
who fought against the U.S. federal
government in an effort to preserve the
traditions and values of the Lakota way
of life.

In Norse mythology, **RAGNARÖK** or
Ragnarök ('Fate of the Gods') is the final
battle waged between the Æsir, led by
Odin, and the various forces of the giants
or Jötnar, including Loki, followed by the
destruction of the world and its subsequent
rebirth. Not only will most of the gods,
giants and monsters involved perish in
this apocalyptic conflagration, but almost
everything in the universe will be torn
asunder and destroyed. What seems
eschatologically unique about Ragnarök
is that the gods know through prophecy
what is going to happen — when the event
will occur, who will be slain by whom, and
so forth.

# WYSE BLOOD

Sebastian Roach

Chapter 1

It first came to her in her sleep, but she was not dreaming at the time, and so was not aware of it. She had woken up feeling troubled by something on that first morning, but did not know by what. She assumed then that it was the same thing that had been troubling her when she had gone to bed the night before. This was, in every sense, a perfectly reasonable assumption, but it was a false one.

The thing that had been troubling her when she had gone to bed the night before had been the fear that she had made a mistake. That this film was not going to be the fun little project, and the change being as good as a rest, that she'd signed up for. Sure, it was low budget and independent, and sure, it was just the kind of quirky, left-field project she'd been telling everyone was what she wanted to do, but there are

limits, you know? There's a point at which quirky becomes just plain weird, and she felt that point had been reached and passed. And she wasn't sure she felt comfortable with that. She certainly felt uncomfortable about something.

When her agent had first told her about it, about this supernatural Western being shot on no budget with the East of England standing in for the Wild West, she had laughed, which she thought was the effect her agent had expected. She thought he'd only told her about it in an attempt to cheer her up at a time when laughing was something she rarely did. He certainly looked surprised when she asked to see the script.

She didn't laugh when she read the script. To be honest she didn't get it, but there was something about it that drew her in, something that grabbed

her and wouldn't let go. Partly it was the simple fact of not getting it. It had been a long time since she'd read a script that challenged her comprehension in a way that left her with the feeling that it was her ability to make sense of the script that was failing, rather than the script's ability to make sense.

Mainly though, the thing that drew her in was the character of Rosie Wilde, the one-eyed showgirl with the heart of tarnished gold and the hands of a killer. It wasn't the part she'd been offered, which brought her up short and made her check back when she came across the words 'flame-haired' in the first line of the character description, but as soon as she read the first line of her dialogue, Rosie's voice was in her head, and it was her own voice, and it said 'I was written for you, even if the writer didn't know it. You were born to play me. I am you, and you are me.'

Even before she'd finished reading, she'd called her agent and said she'd do it, but only if she could play Rosie Wilde. And she'd do it for anything, or for nothing, as long as she played Rosie Wilde.

And so they offered her the part. Well obviously they would, wouldn't they? And they negotiated a fee which was not nothing, but really might as well have been, and that was kind of the point. Money she had. What she hadn't had for a long time was the pleasure of working without the pressure that comes with a multi-million dollar salary, a fifty-foot trailer and assistants with assistants. So to start with, it had all felt so right, and when she'd arrived on location and they showed her where she'd be staying — not a trailer but a cottage, a beautiful old cottage with ivy-covered walls and an overgrown garden — she had a moment of feeling herself almost overwhelmed by a sense of well-being, a rush that left her feeling dizzy, as if the heavy scent of lilies from the garden was going straight to her head.

And that sense of well-being was not tempered — although now she thought, looking back, that perhaps it should have been — when she read the latest draft of the script, which had sweetly been left for her on her pillow. This draft bore little resemblance to the earlier version she'd read, which might have served as an early warning that things could be running out of control, but as most of the changes to the script were geared towards expanding the part of Rosie Wilde and making her more central to the plot, they struck her as both logical and kind of flattering — although it had never been her intention in taking the part that they should change the film to make it all about her.

Even the fact that she could get no cell phone coverage here had seemed, at first, like a positive boon. She'd thought that was amazing — to be

scarcely an hour outside of London and yet utterly remote, almost in a different time entirely. Somehow it made the notion of shooting a Western movie here kind of make sense. Almost.

At the time, at the beginning, it all felt so much like just what she needed. Two weeks of work for the pleasure of the work, no pressure on it, the tranquillity of the countryside and no phone calls. It seemed at first like a spa retreat. Like therapy. Like just what her therapist would have ordered if her therapist had so much as an ounce of common sense in her entire bony body. She decided that first night that this was something else she had to do: when she got home she would start looking for a new therapist, someone who could help her make a fresh start. A clean break. Yes, that was what she needed. The past was the past. It needed to be dead and buried. But it was also that first night that doubts

15

began to creep into her mind, as she lay in bed, unable to sleep.

It was the silence that kept her awake, as much as it was the occasional shriek of some animal or bird that punctuated it. She was a city girl, born and raised, and the only times she had spent any time in the countryside proper she had been insulated from it. When you're there, working on a film with sixty, seventy cast and crew, and you've got twenty-four-hour room service in your country-house hotel, the country doesn't feel very real or very close, it's just the set you're working on. Here, alone in this tiny cottage, the silence and the darkness seemed very real and uncomfortably close. And when, as it was with surprising frequency, that silence was broken by a squawk or a squeal or — even more alarming — a noise that sounded like a human cough, but not human,

it felt quite threatening. She was reminded that out there in the darkness were wild creatures. Beasts. Things that she had no knowledge of. Things she didn't understand.

At night in the city there is always noise and always light. You filter it out, so you are not consciously aware of it, but when it is suddenly taken away, you become aware of how much of a comfort it is to you. A constant reminder that life goes on around you, continuous, and physical, and predictable. At night in the country there are noises in the dark.

She must have fallen asleep eventually that first night because she awoke to a bright shining morning. Sunlight flooded through the pale curtains at her window and birdsong filled the air. She rolled over in bed, closed her eyes and dismissed her night-time doubts with a smile and a shake of the head.

17

She was just a silly little city girl who was afraid
of being alone in the dark. And as for beasts — she
was in Cambridgeshire, not Africa, what beasts do
they have here?

That became the pattern for the first few days.
At night she would be besieged by doubts and
fears. In the morning, with the sunshine, would
come relief, although with each passing night of
disrupted sleep, that relief was slower to come
and less profound. She had hoped that, as she grew
accustomed to the silence and the sudden noises and
the dark, she would come to sleep better and awake
not just relieved, but refreshed. This didn't happen.
She wondered if this was nerves. Stress brought
on by the working methods she was forced to adopt
during the days.

Those first three days they didn't shoot a scene,
they just rehearsed. The director favoured an

improvisational technique, and he would work with
his principal actors, leaving his DP in charge of what
might otherwise have been second unit photography,
except on a film of this budget there was only the
one unit. The sessions felt more like workshops
than rehearsals, in that the director would have
them throw away the pages of the script they were
scheduled to work on and encourage them to run with
their instincts, even if those instincts ran counter
to the meaning of the scene — as she understood
it — as written on the page. In fact, the further
away from the script they got, the happier the
director seemed. It was not a way of working she
was comfortable with. She had always been happier
working to a tight script under a director with a
very clear vision of what he wanted. A control freak,
even, and there was no shortage of those in the
profession. As an actor, she had always felt more
liberated the less she had to think about what she
was doing or saying. And with a tight script, you got

to say great lines — she always worried that if it was up to her to come up with the words she would just say something dumb — and the fear of that made her nervous, which made her stiff, which would tend to come out in her performances, and could also explain those sleepless nights.

Except. Except that wasn't the case here. Yes, she was uneasy with the method, and yes she felt increasingly cut adrift by her director's apparent willingness to go with the flow, but she felt such an affinity with her character, with Rosie Wilde, that she found, once she'd got into a scene, she didn't have to think about what she was doing or what she was going to say at all. The words just came. And the further into a scene she got, it was as if the deeper inside of her she felt Rosie penetrate, and the more the words that came seemed to come directly from Rosie. Her body was merely their conduit, their medium.

She had never experienced anything like this before.
She had always been uncomfortable when she'd
been in the company of other actors and they'd talk
so earnestly about the 'method', and their 'craft'.
She'd always felt instinctively that someone in the
conversation was a fraud, and while her head told
her it was them, her insecure heart told her that it
was herself. And the heart normally won out over
the head. But what she was going through now
certainly felt like what those other actors described.
It made her think — with her head — that perhaps
her heart had been right all along, that she had been
the fraud, and that here, by some weird freak of
circumstance, she had stumbled across her method
and her craft, and was a fraud no longer. But her
heart, ever fickle, would not believe it.

[ · · · ]

SHEZAD>VERITY
ANY WORD FROM THE OUTLAWS?
I'M REALLY LOVING THIS PROJECT — HOW MANY TIMES
DO YOU GET TO ASK THAT IN AN E-MAIL?

# SCENE 02:
# CHOIR
# OUTDOORS
# MINE/
# GRAVEYARD

NUMBERS SLOWLY
MASS (LIKE
SLEEPWALKERS)
TO PERFORM
HYMN(S)

**THE PERFUMED GARDEN** by Muhammad ibn Muhammad al-Nafzawi is a sex manual and work of erotic literature. The book first became widely known in the English speaking world through a translation from the French in 1886 by Sir Richard Francis Burton.

**FILM NOIR** is a cinematic term used primarily to describe stylish Hollywood crime dramas, particularly those that emphasise moral ambiguity and sexual motivation. Hollywood's classic film noir period is generally regarded as stretching from the early 1940s to the late 1950s. Film noir of this era is associated with a low-key black-and-white visual style that has roots in German Expressionist cinematography.

## WYSE BLOOD

Chapter 2

She woke on the morning of the fourth day after another disturbed night and she lay a while, on her back, listening to the birds singing, her eyes lightly closed against the sunlight that flooded the room, so that her vision, while blank, was filled with a blood-tinged golden glow. She had a later start today. It was the first day of actual shooting with the principals but she would not be needed on set until the afternoon. She had make-up and costume fitting, but they'd want to get those cast members who were on the call sheets for the morning scenes out of the way first, so she could stay in bed until at least ten if she wanted, and she did need to catch up on lost sleep. She slowly started drifting off again.

She jerked awake with a sudden sense of anxiety and a clear memory of having

dreamt. She realised, with a certainty that she felt had crept upon her gradually but made itself known suddenly, that the disturbance to her sleep of the night before had not been in lying awake. She had indeed slept, but that sleep had been riven with vivid dreams, dreams that came back to her now only as shattered fragments, void of any sense of narrative or even of clear images, as if of forms not quite materialised, of sounds being made just on the threshold of her hearing. It was more a memory of having dreamt than a recollection of what it was she had dreamt, and a residing sensation of how the dreams had made her feel, which was a tremendous sadness and anxiety bordering on fear, and a sense of loss and longing, for something, but for what she did not know. She felt as if her heart was pounding and she was struggling for breath, but when she pressed her hand to her breast, everything appeared quite normal, so she assumed that too must have been some kind of sense memory of the dream.

Her body ached with tiredness, but she dared not close her eyes again, so she got up and made herself some herbal tea and thought about taking a Xanax for the anxiety. It was still a good three hours before she would be called, so she decided to go out for a walk instead.

It was a beautiful morning. The English countryside displayed itself at its lush, verdant late summer finest. Bees buzzed, blackbirds sang, doves cooed. If she could not find tranquillity here, then tranquillity was simply not to be found. The path she took crossed grassy meadows, skirted fields of wheat, cut through tangled woods and, after a little more than a mile she found herself on the edge of a village, little more than a couple of rows of tiny cottages, a pub, a post office and, at the top of a low, wooded hill, a church. It was here that the path led her.

She reached the church gate and paused. A small frisson of nervousness ruffled the thin veneer of what tranquillity she had found, but she thought nothing of it in that moment, as churches and graveyards had always, for the obvious reasons, made her shudder a little. She smiled to herself in reassurance as she reached for the handle of the gate. But as her hand touched it, she was startled by a sudden cacophony of rooks bursting from the dark trees that bounded the graveyard. She jumped and as she did so, found herself more startled still by the strong sense that someone was calling her name, in a voice all but drowned out by the angry squawking of the birds. She looked all around her, but there was no one in sight. She heard no human voice, only those of the dispersing rooks.

She turned back to the gate. All the rooks had flown away now. All except one, which wheeled up towards the church steeple, then rolled, half folded its wings and swept downwards, pulling out of its dive just inches from the ground and easing up to gently alight on a gravestone, back in the shadow of the tree from which it had come. It cocked its head and turned a beady eye on her.

She hesitated for a moment, feeling caught in the rook's stare, then again reached out for the gate. The rook cawed.

Again she got the feeling someone was calling her name. Again she turned and looked around. Again, there was nobody there. She turned back to the gate. The rook stared at her. She pulled back her hand.

Suddenly, despite the warmth of the mid-morning sun, she felt cold. A shudder ran up from the very base of her spine and she had to clamp her jaw to prevent her teeth from chattering. She wanted to turn away, to go straight home, but something held

her there, drawing her towards the gate, pulling her into the graveyard. She stood frozen, torn between conflicting impulses, her hand hovering, shaking slightly, halfway between her and the handle of the gate.

Finally the hand moved forward, towards the gate. Again the rook cawed. Again she heard, or rather didn't quite hear but felt, a voice calling her name. Again, she looked all around. Again nobody.

She felt faint now as well as cold, dizzy. Her heart pounded in her clenched chest. She couldn't breathe. She wanted to run, but still she was held, her hand hovering over the handle of the gate, until, apparently of its own volition, and quite against her will, it moved decisively to grasp the handle and push the lever down. The gate swung away from her and she felt herself propelled into the graveyard,

as if pushed from behind. She stumbled slightly,
then recovered, and tried to compose herself.
She found herself stepping cautiously, unwillingly
but unstoppably towards the grave from which the
rook still stared at her with unblinking black eyes.
It bobbed up and down on the headstone, its wings
half opened appearing to be agitated, even excited
by her approach, but not alarmed. It certainly did
not appear to be afraid of her, unlike she of it.
She was terrified, but utterly compelled to keep
going. She was now no more than a dozen feet
away from the grave, from the rook. It cawed
again. This time she did not turn to look for the
person calling her name. There was no person,
there was only the rook.

Finally she reached the foot of the grave. The rook
bobbed up and down twice more, then hopped off
the stone and with three or four flaps of its wings

swept up into the tree above the grave, where it
perched, swaying, looking down at her. She looked
back up at it. It cawed again, quietly this time,
calling to her, almost coaxingly. Whatever anger she
had heard in its cry before seemed to have gone.
Was that the bird, or was it just her?

With a shudder she dragged her gaze from that
of the rook and looked at the headstone in front of
her. It was old, rough, covered in grey-green lichen,
the lettering scarcely legible, but she saw it was a
family grave. Here lay Charles and Mary Wyse of
this parish, who had died thirty years apart, she
young, he older, both over a hundred years ago.
There was something else engraved beneath, but it
was obscured by a coarse thicket of grass growing
out of a crack in the foot of the stone. She stepped
forward, knelt down, reached out. She was feeling
cold all over now. Almost numb. Her hand grasped

the thicket of grass, clumsily tore it away, wiped
the dirt and dead vegetation from the carved letters
that were revealed.

'And in loving memory,' the stone said, 'of Rose
Wyse, taken from us aged 8 years. 1854.' That was
eight years on from the death of Mary. Beneath that
was a strange message, clearly meant as a comfort,
but readable as quite the opposite. 'There's a place
for little children,' it said, 'above the clear blue sky.'

She knelt at the foot of the headstone and stared at
it. She felt too weak, too dizzy, too sick and numb
with cold, although she could feel the heat of the
sun on the back of her neck, to even try to get up.
Then the rook cawed again, louder than ever this
time, and she flinched as it swooped down from it's
perch, passing so low over her she felt the rush of
air from the beat of its wings. As it wheeled up and
away over the high hedge, still calling out to her she
realised she was no longer hearing her name. It was
just the call of a bird.

She was released. She forced herself up on hollow-
feeling legs and turned and stumbled, she wanted
to run — but she couldn't — as fast as she could,
out of the churchyard and back down the path. She
dared not look around, not until she reached the foot
of the shallow hill on which the church stood. Here
she stopped to catch her breath.

A blackbird singing was the only bird she could hear
now. Bees hummed. Far in the distance she could
hear a plane. Slowly she turned and looked back
up the hill. There was no sign of anything sinister,
just a pretty, if ordinary, English country church
surrounded by trees at the top of a small hill, under
a blue sky with little fluffy white clouds. Gradually
the tension in her chest eased and her heart rate
slowed to something like normal, but still her breath

came fast and shallow. She turned again and hurried back the way she had come.

The further away from the church she got, and the closer to the security of her cottage, and of other people, the more she became aware of a creeping sense that she was running away. That someone, or something, had been calling to her, beseeching her and she had turned her back. She felt a sense of abandonment on behalf of someone or something that she herself had abandoned without knowing; it was a feeling of regret, of remorse, that became an almost unbearable sadness.

And, suddenly, she found herself thinking about her own lost baby. It had been almost five years ago now, when she was still married, just. She had told him she wanted a divorce, then found out she was pregnant, then had the miscarriage. It really hadn't been that traumatic: she was young; her career was just taking off; it would have been a child she didn't want with a man she no longer wanted to be with. It had happened very early in the pregnancy, in the period in which you're not meant to tell anyone you're pregnant because of the likelihood of just that happening. She had never even told him. People she did tell — her closest friends — said it was the stress of the break up, but she knew it wasn't. She had willed it. The first considered emotion she had felt, after the pain and the fear and the shock of the event itself, was relief. Relief that she didn't have to go through with it, or make the choice not to. Relief that she was free. Of the baby. Of him.

It had taken her a long time to get over, not the grief at the loss of the child — that she hadn't yet come to think of as a child, but the guilt at having been glad.

It had taken a long time to get over it, but she was sure that she had. She hadn't thought about it at all in two, maybe three years. It was silly, she tried telling herself, to have it brought to mind by the death of some other child, some random lost child, over a hundred and fifty years ago. It was absurd.

It was only after she'd been thinking about it for several minutes, long enough to be almost back at the cottage, that she realised she had consciously thought of it, not as her miscarriage, but as her lost baby. She had never done that before.

By the time she reached the cottage, her eyes were filled with tears. She went straight to the cabinet in the bathroom and took that Xanax.

[ · · · ]

# The Old Rugged Cross

GALATIANS 6:14
G. B., 1913

George Bennard, 1913

1. On a hill far a-way stood an old rug-ged cross, The em-blem of suf-f'ring and shame;
2. Oh, that old rug-ged cross, so de-spised by the world, Has a won drous at - trac - tion for me;
3. In that old rug-ged cross, stained with blood so di - vine, A won - drous beau - ty I see,
4. To the old rug-ged cross I will ev - er be true; Its shame and re-proach glad - ly bear;

And I love that old cross where the dear - est and best For a world of lost sin-ners was slain.
For the dear Lamb of God left His glo - ry a-bove To bear it to dark Cal - va - ry.
For 'twas on that old cross Je - sus suf-fered and died, To par - don and sanc - ti - fy me.
Then He'll call me some day to my home far a - way, Where His glo - ry for - ev - er I'll share.

*Refrain*

So I'll cher - ish the old rug - ged cross,_____ Till my tro - phies at last I lay down;
cross, the old rug - ged cross,

I will cling to the old rug - ged cross,_____ And ex-change it some day for a crown.
cross, the old rug - ged cross,

# SCENE 03:
# FIRE
# KRISHNA
# CRAZY HORSE

FIXED CAMERA

PANNING refers to the horizontal movement or rotation of a film or video camera, or the scanning of a subject horizontally on video or a display device. Panning a camera results in a motion similar to that of someone shaking their head 'no'.

The PANOPTICON is a type of prison building designed by English philosopher Jeremy Bentham in 1785. The concept of the design is to allow an observer to observe (-opticon) all (pan-) prisoners without the prisoners being able to tell whether they are being watched, thereby conveying what one architect has called the 'sentiment of an invisible omniscience'.

LONG KNIVES or Big Knives was a term used by American Indians of the Ohio Country to designate British colonists in North America. The origin is thought to have been the swords carried by colonial military officers.

## ON PARTICIPATION IN
## *FEATURE* AS CHIEF CRAZY HORSE
## OF THE OGLALA SIOUX

David Medalla

Many years ago, when I was a young lad, I met an
American Native who lived in Rhinebeck, New York,
who said that my features resembled his fellow
Natives. Originally I come from the Philippines, and
many members of Filipino tribes (including those of my
 parents: the Batanguenos and the Cebuanos) do
resemble American Natives. In my youth, my
brothers and male companions and I cheered
the Filipino patriot named Geronimo, who
defeated the American officer who killed the
famous Geronimo of the Seminole tribe of the
Florida Everglades. We thought it was a form of justice.

The Beatnik poet Greogry Corso told me in the 1960s
in Paris (inside the cell-like room he inhabited at the
Hotel Stella) that Americans like him were always on
the move. According to him they could never settle
peacefully on any piece of land in the United States
for it was inhabited everywhere by the ghosts of
the American Natives massacred by the European
colonialists. I ended up incorporating Gregory Corso's
comments in a dance drama in 1976 during an exhibition
mounted by AIM, the American Indian Movement.
The AIM project coincided with an exhibition of Native

American Art organised by the Hayward Gallery
to celebrate the bicentennial of the founding of the
United States.

One Sunday evening in the year 2006, Shezad Dawood
came to the Angel Pub in central London. The Angel
Pub (next to St. Giles Church, at the bottom of
Denmark Street, behind the tall Centre Point building
on Tottenham Court Road) is a typical old English pub
with a coffered ceiling, with embossed Tudor roses.
Its location near the end of Charing Cross Road and
on the edge of Covent Garden makes it a convenient
meeting venue. The informal meetings of the London
Biennale, a non-institutional free organisation that I
founded with Adam Nankervis in 1998, are held there

and are without fail lively affairs. Conversations are conducted in diverse languages, mirroring the diversity of the artists' backgrounds and artistic practices.

In the midst of these lively discussions, Shezad Dawood talked to me of a film project he was working on. Speaking in a mellifluous voice, Shez asked me if I would like to play the role of Chief <u>Crazy</u> <u>Horse</u> of the Oglala Sioux. It wasn't until much later that I learned that Shez's movie project was a 'Zombie Western', an original genre of film. I welcomed the invitation to participate in this project because for many years I have felt deep sympathy with American Natives.

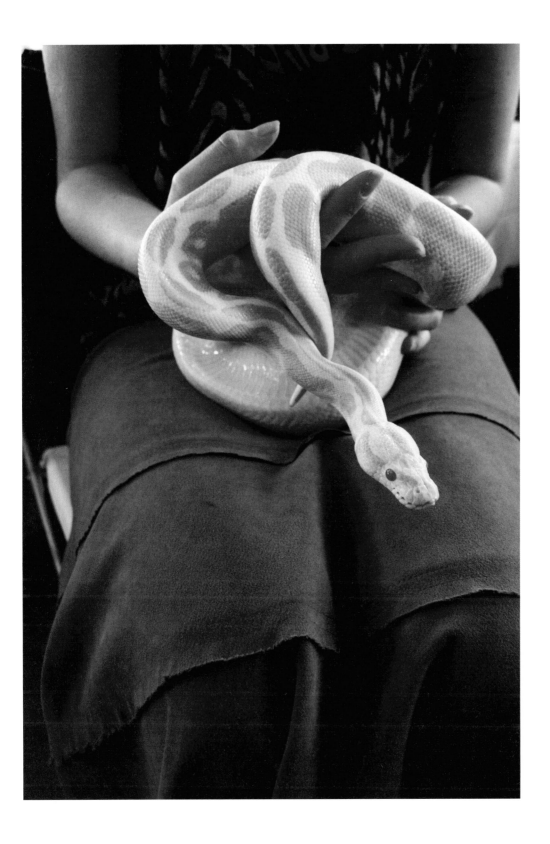

After our conversation at the Angel Pub, Shez arranged for us to meet one day at King's Cross station in London, from where we took a train to Leeds in Yorkshire. Having arrived in Leeds, Shez gave me a bonnet of feathers to wear. I already had a hand-dyed blanket with me that I could wear like a poncho. As soon as we had arrived, Shez told me simply to walk wherever I wanted to, while he filmed me walking. I walked to the shopping centre, to the old market. Sometimes I followed a particular person: a beautiful young lady, a handsome young man, old age pensioners, women shopping, people of different nationalities, of different ages. Kids especially noticed me, thinking perhaps I was a visiting Indian Chief. Some people asked me who I was, while others took no notice of me at all, and I drifted all afternoon through different parts of Leeds like a ghost. Shez said he was satisfied with what we had done that day, and we celebrated with a meal in an Italian restaurant near the hotel where we would stay for the night.

Several months later Shez contacted me again and asked me to meet him at the Diorama Arts Centre near Great Portland Street in London. To continue his film project he had arranged for actors and a film crew to be there. A wooden hut (looking like a garden shed) was constructed inside the arts centre, which was the setting for a bloody scene in the movie. As part of my role I was set upon by treacherous white men (played by the actors, who, in real life together with the crew, were in fact a friendly bunch).

The wooden hut (in which the scene we shot at the Diorama was shown) was presented at the ICA Gallery for the series of six exhibitions entitled *London: Six Easy Steps*. I also participated in one of the shows with a Cosmic Wrestling Match between Adam Nankervis as the Ghost of Joseph Beuys and myself as the Spirit of Marcel Duchamp's Rrose Sélavy. The Spirit of Rrose Sélavy (seductive and erotic) and the Ghost of Joseph Beuys (militant and didactic) were very different from the Ghost of Chief Crazy Horse of the Oglala Sioux (whose plaintive presence is forever linked, in my mind, to the bravery he practised in real life). Those who saw the sequence of Chief Crazy Horse assassinated by the white men, felt horror at the deed and sympathy for the great Oglala Chief.

Gradually the film in which I would take on the role of Chief Crazy Horse began to take shape. The final scene in which I participated took place in a field in Cambridgeshire. This time, the film crew included professional cameramen, lighting and sound technicians, set designers, make-up artists and wardrobe mistresses. Some scenes included live horses. I felt like I was transported through time to the moment of the birth of motion pictures, about which I had read in books. There was full-on catering, which brought back memories of going to the Isle of Dogs many years ago to attend the filming of *Caravaggio*, Derek Jarman's homo-erotic masterpiece

The day I arrived at the set, a group of Chinese young men who lived in Cambridge and belonged to an amateur

football club gathered there as well. It had been a case of serendipity that they had been asked to act as Sioux warriors. Suitably made up, the young Chinese looked like Native American braves. They were the ones I led into battle against the whites.

Also on the set was a man who had brought a live albino snake with him. In the role of Krishna, Shez wrapped the snake around his neck. Sitting beside him on a log, I held in my hand the jawbone of an ass. I learned later that Shez found the fierce-looking jawbone in Texas. Shez as Krishna and I as the Ghost of Chief Crazy Horse engaged in a conversation by means of mudras (hand gestures).

As night descended, enveloping the surrounding countryside in darkness, the war cries of the Sioux braves rose up. They emerged from the shadows: the ghosts of the Sioux warriors, while I, as the ghost of Chief Crazy Horse, wielded the lethal jawbone in my hand, urging them to avenge my death and theirs, as they danced around the blazing fire.

The albino snake around Krishna's neck tried several times to slide down the white jacket of the blue-skinned god. The snake moved excitedly towards the flickering flames of the fire in front of us. When the ghosts of the Sioux warriors vanished into the night, Krishna's blue-coloured face (his forehead marked with a cross) turned gently towards me. He offered me, the ghost of Chief Crazy Horse, the pipe of peace. We took turns inhaling the smoke. Sparks from the fire flickered like stars in the surrounding darkness. The smoke from the peace pipe rose in the air in serpentine wreaths, echoing the undulations of the albino snake. In front of the mandala of flames I fell into a trance: from the  distance, across the vastness of the universe, I heard the cry of <u>Black Elk</u>, the medicine man of the Oglala Sioux, greeting the ghost of Chief Crazy Horse.

This text was written at MUSEUM MAN
at Valparaiso, Chile, on 21 January 2008.

ANDY FOUNTAIN > VERITY
SORRY I HAVEN'T BEEN IN TOUCH: THE GUY WITH
THE BLONDE PYTHON IS ON A TRIP SOMEWHERE
AND CANNOT GET HOLD OF HIM. I HAVE SPOKEN
TO ANOTHER CHAP, WHO OWNS CAMBRIDGE
REPTILES, WHICH IS AT HARWICH JUST UP
THE ROAD AND HE IS HAPPY TO DISCUSS WHAT
YOU NEED.

# SCENE 04: KRISHNA RIDES BULL

**JOSEPH FRANCIS 'BUSTER' KEATON** (4 October 1895 – 1 February 1966) was an Academy Award-winning American silent film comic actor and filmmaker. His trademark was physical comedy with a stoic, deadpan expression on his face, earning him the nickname 'The Great Stone Face.' He has also been called 'The Michelangelo of Silent Comedy'.

A **ZOMBIE** is a reanimated corpse. Stories of zombies originated in the Afro-Caribbean spiritual belief system of Vodou, which told of the dead being raised as workers by a powerful sorcerer. Zombies became a popular device in modern horror fiction, largely because of the success of George A. Romero's 1968 film, *Night of the Living Dead*.

**KRISHNA** is a deity worshipped across many traditions of Hinduism. He is usually depicted as a young cowherd boy playing a flute (as in the *Bhagavata Purana*) or a youthful prince giving philosophical direction (as in the *Bhagavad Gita*).

**SAMUEL BARCLAY BECKETT** (13 April 1906 – 22 December 1989) was an Irish writer, dramatist and poet. Beckett's work is stark and fundamentally minimalist. As a follower of James Joyce, Beckett is considered by many one of the last modernists; as an inspiration to many later writers, he is considered one of the first postmodernists. He is also considered one of the key writers in what Martin Esslin called 'Theatre of the Absurd'.

KRISHNA & DRAG QUEENS/ MUSCLE BOYS RIDE IN WITH ROCKY MOUNTAIN BCKDROP FILLING FRAME

# WYSE BLOOD

Chapter 3      Maybe it was the Xanax, maybe it was the relaxation that comes naturally with closing your eyes and your mind, and sitting back in a chair while others attend to your hair and your make-up, but by the time she was ready to be dressed, in costume, as Rosie Wilde, for the first time other than for fittings, she had found at least the semblance of calmness. Still, though, in the dark recesses of her mind, at the very periphery of her consciousness, something lurked. Something she did her best to ignore, but couldn't quite stop herself being aware of. At least once she was laced into her corset, she had a rational explanation for why she should be finding it difficult to breathe, which in a strange way was rather a comfort.

She was helped into the dress, an elaborate confection of shimmering emerald satin, with a stiff bodice and a frilled fishtail skirt.

The wardrobe mistress called for help — doing it up
was a two-person job, three if you counted the person
wearing it. She held her breath and arched her back
and felt her ribs compress and as each hook met each
eye, working up from the base of her spine, she began
to feel light headed. She closed her eyes, thinking for a
moment she was going to faint.

A voice spoke. Somewhere behind her. She didn't quite
catch it. She opened her eyes and looked in the mirror.
Both the wardrobe mistress and her assistant were
focused intently on her back, their faces showing
the strain that her ribcage was bearing the brunt of.
Neither of them appeared to be expecting an answer
from her.

'I'm sorry?' she said
The wardrobe mistress looked up: their eyes met in the
mirror. 'Sorry? What for?'

'Didn't you say something?'
The wardrobe mistress shook her head. 'No.' The
assistant glanced up too, shrugged. She clearly hadn't
said anything either.

'Oh. I thought you did.' She glanced around, insofar
as she could twist herself at all in the corset and the
dress. There was nobody else in the room.

The wardrobe mistress straightened her up with a
gentle but firm push between the shoulder blades.

'Okay now,' she said. 'Just one more hook and
we're done.'

'You look fabulous,' said the director when she arrived
on set.

'I know,' she said, entirely without vanity. She did

look fabulous — the combination of the emerald green dress and her bright auburn hair and the milk-white complexion the make-up had given her was stunning — but she felt very strange. She had looked in the mirror when they were done, and she hadn't recognised herself. She presumed she recognised Rosie Wilde, and told herself that was a good thing. But she felt she knew Rosie Wilde, and somewhere, deep at the back of her mind, this felt like looking at a stranger.

She put it down to nerves. This was her first scene, after all. She stepped under the lights. The sudden heat made her sway a little.

'You know how we rehearsed this?' The director spoke from behind the camera and directly in front of a klieg light. She had to shield her eyes with her hand to try and see him as he spoke. Something moved. On the very edge of her vision, to her right, outside the circle of light. She glanced that way. Nothing there. She looked back to the director. He was still speaking. She couldn't pick out his face against the light at all now. The thing moved again. This time she turned fully to her right. Again, nothing.

'... so I just wanted you to go with that feeling.' The director stopped talking, she had no idea what he had said. 'Are you okay?'

'Er, yeah,' she said. 'I'm sorry, could I get some water here?'

She blinked into the light. The eyepatch might have come in handy here, but this first scene was a flashback, to before Rosie lost her eye. The eye itself was due to go in the second scene they were scheduled to shoot. That would be the big set piece scene shot later in the evening: this one was a nice simple little scene, a nice warm up for her. Except now, suddenly, she really couldn't remember how they'd rehearsed it. Her mind was a blank.

Someone handed her a bottle of water. The clapper girl. She took a swig. A deep breath.

'So. You ready?' asked the director.

Had she been able to see his face, perhaps she might have been able to say something, to say no, she wasn't ready, to say anything at all. But she couldn't see his face, and try though she did, she couldn't speak. She could have shaken her head, but she didn't. She nodded. Handed the water bottle back to the girl. 'Okay,' called out the director. 'Quiet on set. And camera, roll sound.'

'Rolling.'

'Mark it.'

'Slate twenty-eight. Take one.'

'And... Action!'

And the scene came to her. Utterly without conscious awareness of it. She had no recollection of the original script, or of how they'd rehearsed it, how they'd improvised. Every time the actor she was playing against spoke, it was not a line she knew, or even felt she'd heard before. And yet the words she needed in response just came to her. Not as if scripted, or by any creative act of her own. The words were just there. Rosie knew what to say.

'And cut.'

There was total silence on set. She was aware that everyone was staring at her. She really had very little idea of what she had actually just done, whether it was good or bad. This was unnerving.

'Camera, good?' the director asked. 'Sound?'

The DP and the sound guy both nodded and made approving noises.

'Great, then I think we got it. Let's move on.'

The director moved out from behind the camera now, out from in front of the light. Finally she could see his face. He was grinning, almost giggling in delight.

'That was awesome,' he said. 'So much better than how we rehearsed it. Where did that come from?'

She had no idea. She didn't even know what it was.

'That's what's so great about this,' the director said. 'It's really nothing to do with me. It's beyond my control.' Now he actually did giggle. 'It's like being a spectator at my own funeral.'

She felt faint again. The clapper girl obviously saw her sway, and appeared at her elbow with the bottle of water again.

'That was amazing,' said the girl, as she handed her the opened bottle. 'I had goose bumps.'

She smiled weakly. 'Thank you,' she said.

They moved on. To the scene she had dreaded shooting from the moment she had committed herself. The one scene that had, somehow, remained intact

through all the rewrites, and rehearsals and improvs.
The scene in which Rosie Wilde was run out of town
by a lynch mob. The scene in which she lost her eye
to a bullwhip. The guy with the whip was an expert.
He had proved his accuracy by lining up rows of cans,
tightly spaced, on a wall, and picking off just the one you
pointed to, without disturbing the ones either side of it.
He did it again and again, never missed once. Then they'd
given her a mask, like a fencer would wear, and they'd
done a few run throughs with him cracking the whip at
a piece of paper hung from a wire just eighteen inches
from her face, and every time he hit the piece of paper,
took a tear out of it, never came closer to her face than
that. But every time he did it, she felt, rather than heard,
the whipcrack and was almost sick.

And in the scene, she wouldn't be wearing the mask.
No wonder she'd been feeling anxious all day, she told
herself. What with the whip, and the usual nerves,
and the corset; no wonder she couldn't breath. In a

conventional movie, with a proper budget, they'd have a body double for this sort of thing she thought. Thank god for body doubles.

The director tried to reassure her, explaining how they were cheating the shot, so the guy would actually be cracking the whip further away from her face than it would look on camera, much further away than they had practised with the mask, so really there was nothing to be scared of.

And she tried to be convinced. Really she did. She tried to have faith in the guy with the whip and in what the director was saying, tried telling herself that the fear of the whip was quite rational and perfectly okay, and what with that and the predictable nerves, and the corset, and the flaming torch lit set and the choir of towns folk singing their frankly terrifying hymns with lyrics full of bloody crosses and fountains of blood, and guilt and shame and death, it was no wonder she was

hyperventilating a little. No wonder she felt like she was on drugs.

So she tried to ignore the voices she kept not quite catching, and the things that were constantly moving just outside her field of vision.

And when they came to shoot the scene and the whipcrack came, and again she felt it rather than heard it, a very real pain shot through her eye, and she was convinced she was hit. A searing pain, like a hot knife stabbing clean through her eye and deep into her brain. She stumbled, clutched at her face, pressing her hand to her eye socket, dreading what she might feel — blood, something worse than blood. She screamed in agony, and at the back of her mind — under the scream, or part of the scream, she couldn't tell — could clearly hear the words 'I can't see! I can't see!' She really didn't know if she was actually saying that out loud, or just hearing her thoughts put into words. Or the thoughts of Rosie Wilde.

She was on her knees, being dragged by the arm, by the hair, by the lynch mob. Still the choir sang, about sins being washed away in the blood of the lamb. Still she screamed. Fearfully she pulled her hand from her eye and looked at her palm, with her other, good eye. There was no blood, no lacerated eyeball. She opened the shut eye. She could see. The scream subsided into sobs. She could see.

The director shouted cut. As he did so she again heard the voice, the one she thought she'd heard at the back of her mind, but now it was coming from outside of her, just as much as the director's was.

'I can't see! I can't see!' the voice said again. She knew now it was the voice of Rosie Wilde.

She fell fast into a deep sleep when she reached her bed that night. So exhausted was she by the anxiety and fear of the day, that she no longer felt it. Not consciously. But it returned to her in her dreams. They were vivid, almost lucid dreams, the kind that feel like entirely convincing realities in their own right, and yet at the same time, you are aware, even as you are dreaming them, that they are indeed dreams.

And they were exactly the kind of dreams she would have expected to have: full of torchlight, and whipcracks and the words of those awful, bloodthirsty hymns. And the cawing of rooks and the loud, frantic beating of wings. And running all through the dreams were the sensations both of searching for, and being pursued by, something unknown. Except, for all that she didn't know what it was, it felt like she knew it subconsciously. Something that hovered on the edge of her consciousness like a word on the tip of her tongue. But every time, in the dream, she felt that knowledge was about to be revealed to her, she would wake, sweaty but cold, tangled in her sheet.

And each time she suddenly awoke, despite the unease of her dreaming state, she would almost as quickly fall asleep again, and the dream, or another, similar dream, would recommence.

And there was the voice. Over and over, like a plaintive refrain. 'I can't see,' it would call out. And sometimes, in the dream, it was her calling out, and sometimes it was her hearing the voice, and sometimes it was her voice, and sometimes Rosie Wilde's, and sometimes her as Rosie Wilde, and sometimes her as herself hearing Rosie Wilde. And, more and more, whether it was her or Rosie Wilde, whether she was hearing the cries or calling out herself, it was the voice of a child.

'I can't see,' cried the child. 'Where are you? I can't see you.'

'I'm here,' she called back. 'Here I am.'
And the voices sounded the same to her.

'I can't see!' cried the child.

She was suddenly jerked awake. That cry had surely
been real. It had woken her from her dream, so surely
it had come from outside the dream. A child's voice,
clear as the day that was just breaking. She listened
hard in the half light that was creeping into the room.
A bird — a blackbird though she didn't know it —
started to sing, soon was joined by another, then
another. She sat upright in her bed, her sheet pulled
tight around her, listening for the child's voice that
had called to her from her sleep.

[ · · · ]

VERITY > SHEZAD
I have a lead about a donkey at Shepreth Wildlife Park so will pursue that. The Outlaws may not actually turn up on the Saturday. The choir will be there from 3 pm – 5 pm. I sent Ralph, the conductor, 'There is a Fountain Filled with Blood', 'The Old Rugged Cross', 'Bring in the Sheaves' and 'His Eye is on the Sparrow'. They all seem to be in the public domain in the US, and they probably are here as well.


MANSOOR > VERITY
Shez did suggest that Pete and I come and scope out the field you guys intend to do the horse chase in to see how best to work it.


VERITY > LIZ & TERRANCE
Thank you so much for coming and bringing Daisy along on Saturday. She was fabulous and really stole everyone's hearts. It would be great if you could come back this Saturday with Daisy at 5 pm. It should be another interesting scene as Hetna Regitze of the Danish National Opera will be there and quite a few of the actors will be in full zombie make-up!


LIZ > VERITY
We all enjoyed our visit too, and are very happy to bring Daisy back next Saturday at 5 pm. I hope you don't want her to sing along, she has a VERY LOUD bray!!!

# SCENE 05: BURLESQUE DANCER BAND SALOON

The name **WINCHESTER** rifle is frequently used to describe any of the lever-action rifles manufactured in America by the Winchester Repeating Arms Company in the latter half of the nineteenth century, although it is usually in reference to the Winchester Model 1873 or the Winchester Model 1894. The gun is colloquially known as 'The Gun that Won the West' for its immense popularity at that time, as well as its use in fictional Westerns.

**RONALD MCDONALD** is a clown who is the primary mascot of the McDonald's fast-food restaurant chain. According to the book *Fast-Food Nation* (2001), 96% of school children in the United States can identify Ronald McDonald, making him the United States' most recognised fast-food advertising icon. Only Santa Claus was more commonly recognised. The McDonald's Corporation has also characterised Ronald McDonald as being able to speak 31 different languages including Mandarin, Dutch, Tagalog, and Hindi.

The **BANJO** is a stringed instrument developed by enslaved Africans in the United States, adapted from several African instruments. The name banjo commonly is thought to be derived from the Kimbundu term mbanza. Some etymologists derive it from a dialectal pronunciation of 'bandore', though recent research suggests that it may come from a Senegambian term for the bamboo stick used for the instrument's neck.

FIXED CAMERA ON 'STAGE'

## WYSE BLOOD

Chapter 4

She stood at the side of the set, in costume and fully made-up, waiting for her cue. Breathing was still an effort, but that was just corsetry. She felt calm. She always felt better the second day of shooting, more confident, more relaxed into her role, and, more than that on this occasion, today there had been no voices in her head, and nothing moving just out of her field of vision.

She had felt that calmness growing inside of her with the light of day growing in her room as she had sat in bed, listening to the birdsong. They had just been dreams she had told herself, over and over, with increasing certainty. Just her brain taking the jumble of events and impressions from the previous day and trying to make some kind of sense of it all. None of it meant anything. It was all just dreams.

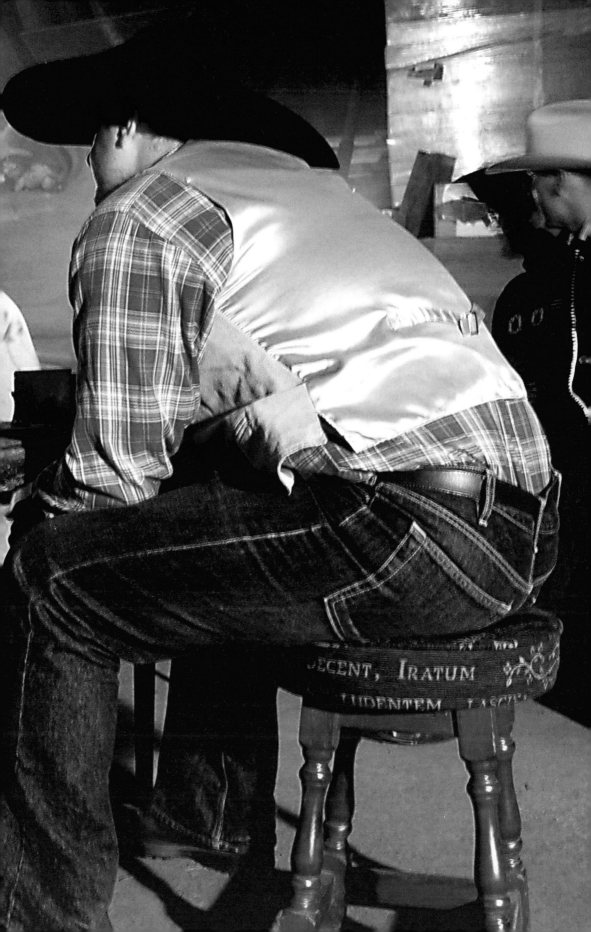

And that calmness had been reinforced by the couple
of hours she had spent sat in her chair, lying back,
eyes closed, being pampered and made-up and
dressed, by real, live, flesh and blood people.

And now she was ready for her scene: calm,
confident, serene, at ease.

Suddenly the wardrobe mistress was at her side,
breathing a little hard.

'We forgot this.' She held up the bejewelled eye
patch, with black ribbons, that completed Rosie
Wilde's costume.

She smiled and ducked her head slightly for the
wardrobe mistress to reach up and round the back
of her head, tie the ribbons and slide the patch down
over her left eye.

A voice whispered. Too low to quite hear,
somewhere behind her. She turned to look, but
there was nobody there, turned back to see the
wardrobe mistress, holding up a mirror for her.
'That was a close one,' she again smiled with a
sheepish shrug.

She pushed the patch back up off her eye.
The whispering stopped.

No longer at ease, she suddenly felt quite, quite cold.
She turned away from the wardrobe mistress and
the mirror, tried to concentrate on the scene being
played in front of her, took a deep breath, as best as
she could, ready for her cue.

And cold though she was already, a new creeping
chill spread rapidly through her. The line that was
her cue, even before it came, had suddenly taken
on a significance she'd never given it before. It had
just been her cue. But now, even before he said it,

when the Sheriff said to the Confederate General, 'Of course, she didn't go by the name Rosie Wilde back then,' she knew, though it was never mentioned in the script, nor had it been suggested in improv during rehearsals, what name it was she had gone by back then.

It was as stone-cold certain to her as anything had ever been, her name, Rosie Wilde's name, had been Rose Wyse.

'Of course, she didn't go by the name Rosie Wilde back then,' the Sheriff said to the Confederate General.

She pulled the patch down over her left eye, and went to step forward, into the light. And she could not. Try as she might, she could not move.

The voice had come back, but it was not whispering now, it was loud, drowning out all other sounds, and yet it still was not clear: she couldn't make out the words. And the lights were suddenly bright, blindingly bright, shining right into her uncovered eye. She closed her eyes, both of them, tight against the light. The voice got instantly clearer. She still couldn't quite pick out the words but she knew the voice, and what it was saying.

It was a child's voice. 'Where are you? I can't see you,' it said.

She opened her eye. The left eye. The patched eye.

It took a few moments for her eye to adjust — strangely she was not sure if it was adjusting to darkness, or to the light, but gradually a figure emerged, poorly defined, shimmering slightly, as if seen through the flame of a candle. The figure of a child, a little girl, maybe eight years old. A little girl with flaming red hair.

Like Rosie Wilde's. Like her own.

'I can see you,' she said, in a voice that was not picked up by the boom mike overhead. The sound man, hearing nothing in his ear phones, did not even glance up. 'I can see you, don't be scared.'

The figure was clearer now, the candlelight steadier, less shimmery, but the child's face remained somehow blurred, as if out of focus, or seen through gauze. She could see that the eyes, though, were huge. Huge and deep and dark.

'I can see you,' she said again. It seemed important.

The child's mouth opened, but no sound came out.

'I can see you,' she said again.

And then she screamed. The sound that came out of her mouth was loud, piercing, blood-chilling. It was certainly picked up by the boom mike. The sound man leapt to his feet, pulling his headphones away from his ears and throwing them away in pain. Everyone else on the set froze. Whatever they were doing, they stopped short and they stared at her.

She did not see them stare. Her uncovered eye was open again but it was not seeing cast or crew, camera or lights. She was seeing something nobody else could, and still the scream came from her mouth. But the voice that screamed was not her own.

[ End ]

1.      'The History of Language is a history of historical reversals, just as a particular flourish gains ascendance, another is pushed to compensate by a sudden $_{nd}$ swift evolution of style. In this way a certain polarity is maintained at a more general level, despite what appear, at least in the short term, as dramatic incursions. This is all the more evident in the shift between mediaeval gothic $_{nd}$ sans serif as a cyclical pattern emerging through the social tensions between the age of chivalry $_{nd}$ its more austere ecclesiastical counterpart, and yet both providing their own advances in arts $_{nd}$ letters. Something like the tension between allegory $_{nd}$ mystery that lies at the heart of cinema noir.'

# SCENE 06: INDIAN VILLAGE FIRE ROAD KILL

Greenhouses

FIXED SHOT

**VOODOO** is a religious tradition originating in West Africa, which became prominent in the New World due to the importation of African slaves. West African Vodun is the original form of the religion; Haitian Vodou and Louisiana Voodoo are its descendants in the New World.

**MICHELANGELO ANTONIONI** (29 September 1912 – 30 July 2007) was an Italian modernist film director whose films are widely considered as some of the most influential in film aesthetics.

**GEORGE ANDREW ROMERO** (born 4 February 1940) is an American director, writer, editor and actor. He is best known for his Dead Series of five horror movies featuring a zombie apocalypse theme and commentary on modern society.

**GEORGE ARMSTRONG CUSTER** (5 December 1839 – 25 June 1876) was a United States Army officer and cavalry commander in the American Civil War and the Indian Wars.

## THE VOYAGE,
## OR, POETRY HAS PROBABLY
## LOST ITS PAST POWER ☻

————Jimmie Durham ☼

☻ Do not worry; this phrase is only an introduction
to the poetic devices used in this poem.

Before we got into this predicament.
Perhaps a classical poetic notion,
But not the words; know, knot the unpoetic English words.

This business language so far from poetry
Yet Percy Shelley and that guy who
Wrote about a wasp chill'd with cold, and
Larkin - - - [Robert Herrick?]

What predicament? Who are 'we'?
Any appropriate shore bird can say,
' Hu-ar-wee-Hu-ar-wee.'

Maria Thereza and me, so strangely
Out of money? So dependent upon
Money? We cannot fish nor forage,
No food without money, no shelter, no
Shirts on our backs, what a predicament!

Or maybe American Indians hung on casinos.
I am going to Sami country in the north, ok,
They've lived there a long time, but now who knows,
Maybe they want to maintain their old ways
On some sunny southern shore?

I mean only that everyone used to be so specific
Out of harsh necessity, and modern mobility
Takes us away from that predicament.
At least allows a cessation of certain
Patterns of repetition.

Perhaps only a cheap poetic device;
That 'we' means me and the paper.
The paper fights to remain white,

Ok, a passive fight, like Gandhi against
My bad English.

I spoke to the architecture students.
' Writing,' I lectured, 'Began in the first city,
The first architecture, made by Gilgamesh
The King and Son of God.'

' Writing and architecture,' the hopeful students were told,
' Replaced memory with law and the sepulchre,
Placed us all against the wall.'
(Hu-ar-wee, Hu-ar-wee)

I write aboard a ship headed north
To Sami country. Two weeks ago I was south;
South as far as Australia, a land called South.
Aboriginals marginal after more than forty
Thousand years of normality such as no one
Else has known.

One year the English came south
And made the Australians aboriginal.
The English made their own Irish prisoners Australian.
(Hu-ar-wee, Hu-ar-wee)

Before we got into this predicament.
Maybe like 'Before the Christian era,' B.C.E.
B.W.G.I.T.P. Before petroleum, perhaps,
Before iron, before fire.

For if comfort is found in universals
' Globalisation' is worthy of this classification
' Predicament'; Isn't it?
(Hu-ar-wee, Hu-ar-wee)

Well is could be art, couldn't it? Or poetry.
Before we got into this predicament art
Happened almost everyday probably,
And poetry tumbled lightly off - - -
Off English words, peut-être.

Well, it could be fire, aboard ship I've begun
To read *Soul Mountain* by Gao Xingjian.
The character seems to search the 'out back'
For more authentic situations, and someone
Prays to a cook stove.

Poet's note:

A few years ago I was in the Republic of Yakutia in Siberia,
which, without a railroad or highway system, and therefore
no Russian Gulag, had become the richest part of the ex-
Soviet Union. They had all become scientists. By this method
they could freely stay at home or travel to work in other
places and Yakutsk culture was neither threatened nor a
burden. Then came along this hijo de puta (Ras) Putin. I've
read that up here (as I write we are close to Russia and to the
North Pole) the old Tsar moved some communities of Nenets
here next to Finland. Then they had to be resettled about
seventy-five years later because of nuclear testing.

What I mean is, by whose authority were those people
'Nenets'? On their own, couldn't they have been just as
important as anyone else, even if they spoke Nenet? I bet
they also spoke Russian, and even Finnish for a while.
If only vulgar guns and power decide who's who, humanity
is seriously degraded. If those with money have privilege
and poor people have few rights, where is humanity?

(Hu-ar-wee, Hu-are-wee)

Before we got into this predicament,
Before vulgar power shot from guns,
Before 'Skallo', the Nordic tax collector.

Aboard this ship I have stopped reading Gao
And now read *Austerlitz* by the dead Sebald;
The predicament might be only a dream
Just as sleep ends, abruptly to the sound
Of freight offloaded.

Any corrupt language which contains
Such beauty as the word 'abruptly' is
Perhaps structurally appropriate.

☼ Coast of Norway, Courtesy Arve Opdahl,  El Pescator

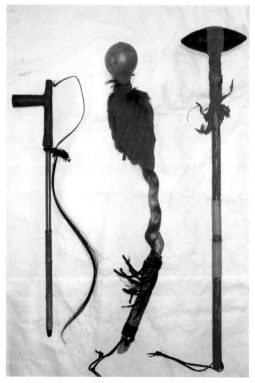

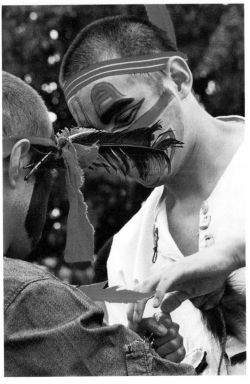

Luong > Verity
My name is Luong and we do have an Oriental
based (generally Chinese) football team
that might be interested if you could supply
me with more details. I also personally
know a fair few Oriental people in and
around Cambridge. The other contact I have
is for Jason Yow, the head of the Chinese
Community Centre, but he is generally quite
busy and the community centre is typically
for the older generation.

Shezad > Verity
Been reading about common theory that
native Americans originated in China, via
pre ice-age land bridge... maybe we should
have them as Indians, go for it!

Ralph Woodward > Verity
I've sounded out the committee and they're
on board and happy to negotiate with
you, so I've sent an invite to the choir.
Responses are dribbling in this morning,
but it's looking likely that we'll get
30ish. I'll be able to tell you the gender
split for costume purposes soon.

Andy Dunbar > Verity
Regarding the build tasks, it all looks
fine so far. Areas that might incur extra
costs are: Indian Village – teepee building
materials (rolls of calico and some lengths
of wood). Battle of Little Bighorn – cost
for replacing wagon if burned, or to
build one specifically to set fire to,
plus material to make the peace pipe and
bows and arrows. Wild West town outside
shot – wood glue, paint and wood shavings
to cover. Flat pack building in stock.
Mineshaft – we should be able to do this
with materials available, but may need some
additional wood for graveyard. In addition
we may need a generator and we can provide
a coffin for an additional amount.

# SCENE 07: BATTLE OF LITTLE BIG HORN

EPIC FIXED SHOT

The **MALTESE FALCON** is a 1930 detective novel by Dashiell Hammett, originally serialised in the magazine *Black Mask*. The story has been adapted several times for the cinema. The main character, Sam Spade, appears only in this novel and in three lesser known short stories, yet is widely cited as the crystallising figure in the development of the hard-boiled private detective genre — Raymond Chandler's character Philip Marlowe, for instance, was strongly influenced by Hammett's Spade.

The **BATTLE OF THE LITTLE BIGHORN** — also known as Custer's Last Stand, and, in the parlance of the relevant Native Americans, the Battle of the Greasy Grass—was an armed engagement between a Lakota-Northern Cheyenne combined force and the 7th Cavalry of the United States Army. It occurred between 25 and 26 June 1876, near the Little Bighorn River in the eastern Montana Territory. The battle was the most famous action of the Indian Wars, and was a remarkable victory for the Lakota and Northern Cheyenne. A sizeable force of U.S. cavalry commanded by Lieutenant Colonel George Armstrong Custer was defeated; Custer himself was killed in the engagement along with two of his brothers.

**ARTHUR MACHEN** (3 March 1863 – 15 December 1947) was a leading Welsh author of the 1890s. He is best known for his influential supernatural, fantasy, and horror fiction. He also is well-known for his leading role in creating the legend of *The Angels of Mons.*

# Film fun in the Wild East

■ WORDS: KATHERINE PATEMAN
■ PICTURES: WARREN GUNN

MOVIE hopefuls queued eagerly for their chance to star in a Western film.

Wannabe cowboys and Indians flocked from across the county to the Wysing Arts Centre which had been transformed into a Wild West set complete with painted backdrops, mineshafts and wagons.

More than 150 members of the public were given the chance to try out for the film, and were also able to watch scenes being filmed.

Experimental filmmaker Shezad Dawood is behind the project, which is set to offer a twist to the traditional spaghetti western.

Donna Lynas, director at Wysing Arts Centre, said: "People really got to see what it is like behind the scenes. Those who auditioned really got into it and improvised some fantastic scenes, it was incredible really."

Filming will continue at Wysing throughout September, before the film – called Feature – is unveiled next year.

It will then be shown at the Cambridge Film Festival before it is released to cinemas nationwide.

Ms Lynas added: "It was a really lovely day, a surreal experience. We wanted people to see that art can be challenging, but it can also be fun."

The event is the first held at Wysing, in Bourn, for almost a year, as the centre is currently closed for a major refurbishment.

Its next event is scheduled for January, when the centre is expected to be fully reopened.

katherine.pateman
@cambridge-news.co.uk

CAMERA, ACTION: Scenes during film production. Left, Shezad Dawood directs.
Pictures: 434387, 434389, 434390, 434391.

VERITY > INDIANS

I KNOW LUONG HAS BEEN TRYING TO PERSUADE ALL YOU GUYS TO COME ALONG THIS SUNDAY TO PLAY SOME NATIVE AMERICAN INDIANS IN OUR FILM. I HOPE YOU WILL ALL COME AND JOIN IN THE FUN. WE NEED APPROXIMATELY 10 PEOPLE TO BE THE INDIANS AND WE WOULD APPRECIATE ALL THE HELP WE CAN GET! THE MORE THE MERRIER REALLY. WE NEED YOU TO ARRIVE AT 10.30 AM IF POSSIBLE SO WE CAN GET EVERYONE THROUGH WARDROBE.

THIS WEEKEND IS THE BIG BATTLE SEQUENCE. WE ARE FILMING A SCENE WITH A DANISH OPERA SINGER ON THE SATURDAY AND THEN THE FUN BEGINS ON SUNDAY… WE WANT LOTS OF YOU GUYS RUNNING AROUND PLAY FIGHTING (FLYING KICKS WELCOME!) WITH THE COWBOY/ ZOMBIES. THERE WILL BE BIG BANGS AND LOTS OF SHOUTING SO I HOPE YOU'RE UP FOR IT. WE'RE ALSO GETTING SOME HORSES FOR A CHASE SEQUENCE (ALTHOUGH I'M NOT SURE YOU GUYS WILL BE INVOLVED IN THAT!)

ANYWAY, IT SHOULD BE FUN AND WE ARE RELYING ON YOU COMING ALONG AND TAKING PART. WE ARE PROVIDING FOOD AND SNACKS AND THERE WILL BE LOTS OF INTERESTING PEOPLE THERE AND THINGS HAPPENING — MORE SO IF YOU SHOW UP! I AM SURE WE CAN ARRANGE FOR SOME PEOPLE TO KEEP THEIR TOPS OFF!

2.  'The Rotating camera or image – variously the pan or panoptikon to go back to their linguistic antecedents – always make me refer back to Arthur Machen's *Great God Pan* when thinking of the interplay of time distortion $^{a}_{nd}$ fetish which embodies the operation of the movie theatre. In his *Film* with Buster Keaton, Samuel Beckett typically enough uses the constantly panning camera as a visual pun that at the same time neutralises the comedic aspect of slapstick, leaving only the void at the heart of Vaudeville.'

# SCENE 08:
# ZOMBIE SCENE
# OUTDOOR +
# IN SALOON

## ELIZABETH TAYLOR

Dame Elizabeth Rosemond Taylor, DBE (born 27 February 1932) is a two-time Academy Award-winning English-American actress. Known for her acting skills and beauty, as well as her Hollywood lifestyle, including many marriages, she is considered one of the great actresses of Hollywood's golden years, as well as a larger-than-life celebrity. The American Film Institute named Taylor seventh among the Greatest Female Stars of All Time.

Taylor appeared in her first motion picture at the age of nine for Universal. They let her contract drop, and she was signed with Metro-Goldwyn-Mayer. Her first movie with that studio was *Lassie Come Home* (1943), which drew favourable attention. That movie starred child star Roddy McDowall, with whom Elizabeth would share a lifelong friendship. After a few more movies, the second on loan-out to 20th Century Fox, she appeared in her first leading role and achieved child star status playing Velvet Brown, a young girl who trains a horse to win the Grand National in Clarence Brown's movie *National Velvet* (1944) with Mickey Rooney. *National Velvet* was a big hit, grossing over US$4 million at the box-office, and she was signed to a

long-term contract. She attended school on the Metro-Goldwyn-Mayer lot and received a diploma from University High School in Los Angeles on 26 January 1950, the same year she was first married at age 18. Elizabeth Taylor won the Academy Award for Best Actress in a Leading Role for her performances in *BUtterfield 8* (1960), which co-starred then husband Eddie Fisher, and again for *Who's Afraid of Virginia Woolf?* (1966), which co-starred then-husband Richard Burton and the Supporting Actress Oscar-winner, Sandy Dennis. Taylor was nominated for *Raintree County* (1957) with Montgomery Clift, *Cat on a Hot Tin Roof* (1958) with Paul Newman, and *Suddenly, Last Summer* (1959) with Clift, Katharine Hepburn and Mercedes McCambridge.

Natasha Lawes > Verity
It's a difficult one really. Asking how much it costs is like asking how much is a piece of string! One could create a zombie with a bit of pale make-up and blood or go the whole hog with the half face missing with guts & brains hanging out!

I have been mulling over ways to do the zombie make-up that looks fantastically gorey, but is not too expensive. I am thinking of making sort of half face masks out of silicone that will then blend into the actors' faces with the help of extra gore.

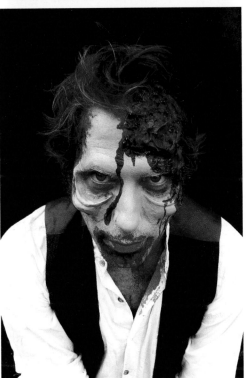

127

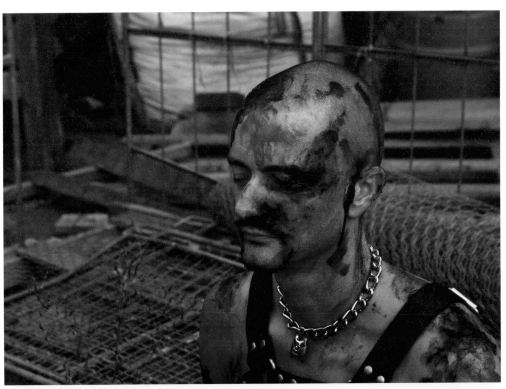

129

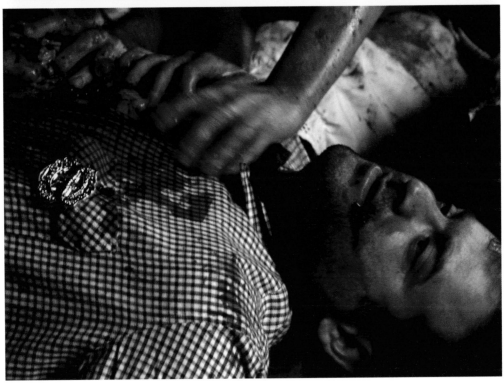

# SCENE 09:
# KRISHNA
# MEDITATING

The **ASHOKA CHAKRA** is a depiction of the Dharmachakra, the Wheel of Dharma. The twenty-four spokes in this chakra wheel represent twenty-four virtues: love, courage, patience, peacefulness, kindness, goodness, faithfulness, gentleness, self-control, selflessness, self sacrifice, truthfulness, righteousness, justice, mercy, graciousness, humility, empathy, sympathy, godly knowledge, godly wisdom, godly moral, reverential.

The **EYE OF PROVIDENCE** or the all-seeing eye is a symbol showing an eye surrounded by rays of light or a glory, and usually enclosed by a triangle. It is sometimes interpreted as representing the eye of God keeping watch on humankind, fear of God AND hope/trust/faith in the goodness of God.

**THE GREAT GOD PAN** is a novella written by Arthur Machen. The original story was published in 1890, and Machen revised and extended it in 1894. On publication it was widely denounced by the press as degenerate and horrific because of its decadent style and sexual content. Machen's story was only one of many at the time to focus on Pan as a useful symbol for the power of nature and paganism.

**SITTING BULL** (ca. 1831 – 15 December 1890) was a Hunkpapa Lakota Sioux holy man, born near the Grand River in South Dakota and killed by police on the Standing Rock Indian Reservation during an attempt to arrest him and prevent him from supporting the Ghost Dance movement. He is notable in American and Native American history for his role in the major victory at the Battle of the Little Bighorn against Lt. Col. George Armstrong Custer and the U.S. 7th Cavalry Regiment on 25 June 1876, where Sitting Bull's premonition of defeating the cavalry became reality.

HE LOOKS ROUND
AT ARROW IN HIS
FOOT.

Tim Sidell > Shezad
Great to meet with you yesterday to discuss your
'Western' project — I'm glad to be on board. I've
attached a Word document with a little table
containing the info that we established yesterday
— perhaps you could coordinate with Verity to
expand this and develop a shot list… I'll look at
the references we discussed and start to formulate
a shooting approach (regarding number of cameras,
format and lighting).

Tim > Shezad + Verity
Shez – here's my understanding of the
elements of action that you need covered:

- Zombies Rise in Battlefield
- Valkyrie starts Aria
- 'Thriller' video with Valkyrie + Zombies
- Krishna CU with gun (blue hand)
- Zombie is shot and falls (arm blows off?)
- 2 Zombies go down
- Pile of dead Zombies
- Valkyrie and Krishna Face-Off
- Valkyrie and Krishna ride off into sunset

        Could you correct/embellish this
shot list and let me know how much of this
you'd like to run as one scene — all of it
(except sunset)? If so, we should probably
reconstruct for a few close-ups (e.g.
Krishna hand with gun + perhaps Valkyrie
starting to sing) as we won't have the cover
of darkness and smoke to hide my roving
steadicam from the wide shot as we did in
the saloon. Or could we plan to run the
whole scene two or three times:
1st) a wide [static] shot from camera on
tripod — a close-up (travelling) shot from
camera on tripod
2nd) a close-up [travelling] shot from
camera on + steadicam
3rd) specific CU's
        I think we should also shoot the
Krishna/crazy Horse scene before dinner as
light is fading fast now — the scene will
have a lot more atmosphere if we can see a
little more than faces. So could we move
this to 6-7 pm, then dinner at 7 pm?


Tim > Kai
Shez and I have decided to shoot S16mm
for the first weekend, then HDV with 35mm
lenses for the second and third weekends.
It's actually during those two later
weekends that we could really use your
help — between focus pulling and operating
— and it'd be great if you could help with
lighting the main Saloon scene during the
second weekend too.

3.      'At the end all are undone, even our hero is forced to abandon his feckless paramour for the isolation of the shadows, of the city. In microcosm suggesting the dual paradigm of Valhalla in Norse mythology, which functions as the abode of Gods and heroes while at the same time doomed to crumble at the end of time, when the dead will walk — known to the Vikings as Ragnarök. 'Ragnarök' representing the end of the world is not far from the notion of time in cinema, which both recurs and undercuts the more widespread illusion of time. Often described in the early Vedic texts of the Indian subcontinent, time is really the locus of the feeble-minded. Hence the appetite for sexual inquiry and storytelling in the Oriental mindset. These high-points of cinematic metaphor operate as cinema out-of-time. With *The Perfumed Garden* first translated by Sir Richard Burton as distinct from the actor who was multiply married to Elizabeth Taylor.'

# SCENE 10:
# BACK TO THE
# BATTLEFIELD
# ZOMBIES RISING
# WOMAN

In Norse mythology the **VALKYRIES** (Old Norse Valkyrja, 'Choosers of the Slain') are dísir, minor female deities, who served Odin. The valkyries' purpose was to choose the most heroic of those who had died in battle and to carry them off to Valhalla where they became Einherjar. This was necessary because Odin needed warriors to fight at his side at the preordained battle at the end of the world, Ragnarök.

**VALHALLA** (Old Norse Valhöll, 'Hall of the Slain') is Odin's hall in Norse mythology, located in the Asgardian realm of Gladsheim and is the home for those slain gloriously in battle (known as Einherjar) who are welcomed by Bragi and escorted to Valhalla by the valkyries.

**FILM** is a film written by Samuel Beckett, his only screenplay. It was filmed in New York in July 1964. Beckett's original choice for the lead — referred to only as 'O' — was Charlie Chaplin, but his script never reached him. The director Alan Schneider was interested in Zero Mostel but he was unavailable. Beckett was 'enthusiastically in favour' of Jack MacGowran as a replacement but he also became unavailable. James Karen, who was to have a small part in the film, talked constantly about the 68 year-old Buster Keaton and persuaded Schneider to consider him when MacGowran's circumstances changed. Schneider credits Beckett himself with the suggestion however.

**ILLUMINATI** is a name that refers to several groups, both real and fictitious. Historically, it refers specifically to the Bavarian Illuminati, an Enlightenment-era secret society founded in the late-eighteenth century. However, in modern times it refers to a purported conspiratorial organisation which acts as a shadowy power behind the throne, allegedly controlling world affairs through present-day governments and corporations, usually as a modern incarnation or continuation of the Bavarian Illuminati. In this context, Illuminati is often used in reference to a New World Order (NWO). Many conspiracy theorists believe the Illuminati, or the 'Illuminated ones', are the masterminds behind events that will lead to the establishment of such a New World Order.

HELEN > VERITY
ONE GOOD THING: THE BATS ARE A NURSERY COLONY
SO THEY MATE AND THEN MOVE ON SO HOPEFULLY THEY
WILL BE OUT COMPLETELY BY THE END OF AUGUST —
SUBJECT TO WEATHER AND TEMPERATURE AND MATING
CYCLES OF BATS!!!

ANNA MELKERSSON > SHEZAD & VERITY
VALKYR: IF THE HELMET DOESN'T FIT, YOU CAN MAKE A
LITTLE CUT IN THE BACK. BUT I HAVE THE SAME HEAD
SIZE, AND IT'S O.K. ON ME. THE BELT IS O.K. ON THE
HIPS OR ON THE WAIST. IT'S NOT SO EASY TO MAKE A
BRA FOR SOMEONE YOU CAN'T MEET — SO I OPTED FOR
PAINTING ON THE DRESS. HOPE IT FITS. I LIKE THE
IMAGE OF THE VALKYR WITH A SWORD IN HER HANDS,
HOLDING IT ON HIP-HEIGHT.
        TEETH NECKLESS MAN: WEAR THE SHIRT
OUTSIDE THE TROUSERS. THE BLACK HAT WITH THE BLACK
FEATHER GOES WITH THIS OUTFIT. THE TEETH ARE A BIT
SENSITIVE, THINK WE BROKE A COUPLE WHEN WE DID
THE PHOTO SHOOT, BUT I THINK IT STILL LOOKS O.K.
THE AXE IS ALSO GOOD WITH THIS OUTFIT. SIZE: QUITE
TALL, GUESS IT'S M/L.
        SHAMAN: THE PIPE IS A BIT SENSITIVE,
ELASTIC PIECES HOLD UP THE SLEEVES. THE SHAMAN
DRUM LOOKS GREAT WITH THIS OUTFIT. SIZE: M/L.
        FEATHER VEST: BIG AND SHORT. THE SHIRT IS
OPEN ON THE SIDES, SO IT COULD FIT A BIGGER PERSON.
THE TROUSERS HAVE ELASTIC FABRIC AT THE WAIST, USE A
BELT TO HOLD THEM UP, CAUSE THEY STRETCH QUITE A BIT.
        CROUCHED FIGHTER: THE ARM LEATHER PIECES
GO ON THE UPPER ARM, TIE THEM WITH THE LACE ON THE
INSIDE. THE BELT HAS THE SAMI WATER BAG ATTACHED
USING THE STRING. LOOKS GOOD IF THE BAG IS ON
THE SIDE.

# FIN

# FEATURE

CAST

_____

SITTING BULL ............................... JIMMIE DURHAM

CRAZY HORSE ............................... DAVID MEDALLA

SHERRIFF ........................................ DOUG FISHBONE

VALKYRIE ........................................ HETNA REGITZE BRUUN

BILLY THE KRISHNA ....................... SHEZAD DAWOOD

GENERALS CUSTER ...................... ⎡ WOLFE LENKIEWICZ
⎢ NIGEL PRICE
⎣ NICK WHITE

MISS ROSIE COOPER ..................... AS HERSELF

MARIACHI ....................................... MIKE CHAVEZ-DAWSON

SCOUT/ZOMBIE ............................ PETE KIRKBRIDE

CHILD/ZOMBIE .............................. ETHAN NESTOR

ZOMBIE BARGIRLS ........................ ⎡ ALEXANDRA MCGUINNESS
⎣ JESSIE FORTUNE RYAN

COWBOY/ZOMBIE ........................... JEREMY ANDREWS

INDIAN GIRL ...................................... ⎡ LAURA MARIA
⎣ VELASQUEZ GUILLEN

INDIAN BRAVE ................................. MANSOOR ABULHOUL

FETISH COWBOYS ........................... ⌠ JULIAN SANDY
                                              │ SIMON TAYLOR
                                              │ STEVE COUSSENS
                                              ⌡ JAMES HOUSE

THE OUTLAWS ............................... ⌠ STUART BIRT
                                              │ LYNN BIRT
     │ LEROY BROWN
     │ FIONA ROSS
     │ SID GUAGE
     │ PETE WILLIS
     │ LIAM RIACH
     │ MIKE HATLEY
     │ KATH BALDWIN
     │ HARRY BALDWIN
     ⌡ PAM HARRIS

EXTRAS .............................................. ⌠ MACK MALTHOY
     │ SIMON MULLEW
     │ N. WOLMARK
     │ RISHI NAG
     ⌡ BRIAN RODGER

COWBOYS/COWGIRLS/ZOMBIES.. ⌠ KIERON WALKER
     │ KEIR HICKMAN
     │ KEVIN MALLEY
     │ ANGELA BANGHAN
     │ ANDREW CONNELL
     │ KAISA PRICEE
     │ ANDY DUNBAR
     │ ROSS PALERSON
     │ VARNA AMJAD
     │ THOMAS E. HANCOCKS
     │ SEBASTIAN ROACH
     │ ANDREW CRAWFORD-
     ⌡ WHITE

INDIANS ........................................... THE CAMBRIDGE
     CHINESE COMMUNITY CENTRE
     FOOTBALL TEAM:
     ⌠ LUONG TRAN
     │ CHUNG TU
     │ CUONG DANG
     │ BE DOAN
     │ MICHAEL CHAN
     │ MINH PHUNG
     │ GEOFFREY CHOW
     ⌡ JAMES YU

CHOIR/TOWNSPEOPLE ................. THE FAIRHAVEN SINGERS
CONDUCTED BY ............................... RALPH WOODWARD

THE BAND ........................................ THE LONESOME COWBOYS
     FROM HELL
     FRANK E.
THE LONELY WOODSMAN ............ CALUM F. KERR
BLIND 'GENTLEMAN' JK-EE........... TIM FLITCROFT
RODEO MARCO ............................... MARC VAULBERT DE CHANTILLY

AND TO THEIR ABSENT FRIEND AND LEADER
JOHN E. CASHMONEY (NIK HOUGHTON 1955–2006)

DAISY THE DONKEY

```
DIRECTOR          .........................................  SHEZAD DAWOOD

DIRECTOR OF PHOTOGRAPHY......  TIM SIDELL

PRODUCER          .......................................  VERITY P. YEATES

EDITOR            ...............................................  BRIAN WELSH

SOUND DESIGNER    ..........................  EMANUELE COSTANTINI

ASSISTANT DIRECTOR    ..................  HOLLY RACE

SECOND ASSISTANT DIRECTOR...  JOANNA MCPHEE

FILM LONDON PRODUCER ............  PINKY GHUNDALE

FILM LONDON HEAD OF
PRODUCTION        .....................................  MAGGIE ELLIS

STILLS PHOTOGRAPHY  ................  ⌈ CHRIS ROGERS
                                      │ LISA BYRNE
                                      ⌋ LEWIN ST. CYR

COSTUME DESIGNER  .....................  ANNA MELKERSSON

MAKE-UP DESIGNER.......................  NATASHA LAWES

MAKE-UP ASSISTANTS ..................  ⌈ VIENNA MCMAHON
                                      │ CHERI PECK
                                      │ ANNICK WOLFERS
                                      ⌋ FAYE QUINTON

FOCUS PULLER/2ND/
3RD CAMERA        ...................................  ⌈ JOSE RUIZ
                                                     │ ANNA BOGACZ
                                                     │ TREVOR SPEED
                                                     ⌋ TONY POWELL

SOUND RECORDING   ......................  ⌈ EMANUELE COSTANTINI
                                          ⌋ FRANCIS CULLEN

TITLES            .............................................  ÅBÄKE

POSTPRODUCTION FACILITY ......  PRIME FOCUS, LONDON
D.I. PRODUCER     .............................  REUBEN GOODYEAR
CONFORM (SMOKE OPERATOR) ...  FRASER CLELAND
COLOURIST (TELECINE)  .............  JAMES TILLETT

SET DESIGN ᵃⁿᵈ CONSTRUCTION..  ⌈ MANDALA STUDIOS:
                                │ ANDY 'FAT GOTH' DUNBAR
                                │ MARK 'WOOKIE' NICHOLS
                                │ NIGEL PRICE
                                │ ANDY 'BLEEDER'CHATWIN
                                │ BEN HESKETH
                                ⌋ TERRY 'TIN' PARSONS

PROPS             ....................................  JOSH SMITH AT GUNMAN

SCENE PAINTERS    ...........................  FAIZ RAHI ᵃⁿᵈ HIS STUDIO

CASTING DIRECTOR  ........................  NADIA VON CHRISTIERSON
```

VOLUNTEERS ................................. 
| RUTH MCPHEE
| SARAH MONSELL
| HANNAH NEWMAN
| SARAH LUDEMANN
| ALEXANDRA MEDEVILLE
| ADELINE WALDRON
| CHLOE JEFFRIES
| DAVINIA BYE
| GEMMA ODDY
| ELLA MCCARTNEY
| ALISON MCTAGGART
| SOPHIA OLEMAN
| FLORA MCLAW
| KATE PRYKE
| ANNA ELGAR
| FRASER STEWART
| MANTO LOURANTAKI
| VERONICA KAVASS
| HELEN JUDGE
| JENNIFER ROBINSON
| NATHALIE ROCHE

————————————————————————————————

WE WOULD LIKE TO THANK

WYSING ARTS CENTRE ................. 
| DONNA LYNAS
| GARY WOOLLEY
| HELEN ROBINSON
| ANDREW CRAWFORD-WHITE
| SARAH EVANS
| ANNE-MIE MELIS

PAUL and ANNE GILDERSLEEVE
FOR THE USE OF THEIR BARN

STUART BIRT AND
THE OUTLAWS

NEIL HARRIS AND
CAMBRIDGE REPTILES

MR and MRS HUGHES FOR THE
USE OF THEIR BULLS

THE CAMBRIDGE CHINESE
COMMUNITY FOOTBALL TEAM

FAIZ RAHI and HIS STUDIO,
KARACHI, PAKISTAN

MANSOOR ABULHOUL FOR
THE USE OF HIS HORSES

LIZ and TERRANCE WHEELER
and LIZ WRIGHT FOR ALLOWING
DAISY THE DONKEY TO APPEAR

PINKY GHUNDALE AT FILM
LONDON FOR VALUABLE
ADVICE AND SUPPORT

FEATURE RECEIVED FUNDING FROM
ARTS COUNCIL ENGLAND EAST AND
WYSING ARTS CENTRE AND WAS
REALISED WITH COMPLETION
FUNDING FROM ARTS COUNCIL
ENGLAND LONDON AND THE
SUPPORT OF FILM LONDON ARTISTS'
MOVING IMAGE NETWORK AND
FURTHER SUPPORT FROM THE
ARTS and HUMANITIES RESEARCH
COUNCIL.

ORIGINAL SCORE COMPOSED BY DUKE GARWOOD

*I Want Too*
written and performed by artist
Mike Chavez-Dawson

*Billy Krishna's Theme*
performed by
Duke Garwood, with Paul May
and John Richards
written by Duke Garwood

*We Are The Lonesome Cowboys*
performed by
The Lonesome Cowboys From Hell
Lyrics by Nick Houghton
Music by Tim Flitcroft

*Post Post Modern Blues*
performed by
The Lonesome Cowboys From Hell
Lyrics by Nick Houghton
Music by Tim Flitcroft

*Stick'em Up Clowns*
performed by
The Lonesome Cowboys From Hell
Lyrics by Calum F. Kerr
Music by Tim Flitcroft

*Moose Catcher*
Written and Performed by
Duke Garwood

*Painting on the Wall*
performed by
The Lonesome Cowboys From Hell
Lyrics and Music by Tim Flitcroft

*Loose Pommade*
performed by
Duke Garwood and Paul May
written by Duke Garwood

*Song of the String*
written and performed by
Duke Garwood

*Bobulu*
performed by
Duke Garwood and Paul May
written by Duke Garwood

*From The Valkyrie*: Sieglinde's aria
*Du bist der Lenzand Brünnhilde's Hojotoho*
Performed by soprano Hetna Regitze Bruun
Lyrics and Music by Richard Wagner

*Billy Krishna's Theme Vol. 2*
performed by Duke Garwood and Paul May
written by Duke Garwood

Published and distributed by Book Works,
London, in collaboration with Castlefield Gallery,
Manchester and Wysing Arts Centre, Bourn, in
association with Leeds Met Gallery, Leeds and
Eastside Projects, Birmingham

ISBN 978 1 906012 08 3
*Fabrications* Editor: Gerrie van Noord
Design: Åbäke, London
Printing and binding: Die Keure, Bruges

*Feature: Reconstruction* is the fifth in a series of
co-publishing partnerships, entitled *Fabrications*,
initiated by Book Works. Book Works is supported
by Arts Council England. *Fabrications* is
supported by National Lottery through Arts
Council England.

Book Works
19 Holywell Row
London EC2A 4JB
www.bookworks.org.uk

*Feature: Reconstruction* is supported by the
National Lottery, through Arts Council England,
the Arts and Humanities Research Council, and
additionally by Wysing Arts Centre and the
Centre for Research and Education in Arts and Media
(CREAM) at the University of Westminster

Thanks to the photographers who contributed the
many images to this book, including: Sophie Aston,
Sarah Evans, Warren Gunn/Cambridge News,
Alexandra Medeville, Sebastian Roach, Jesper
Torsson, Marc Vaulbert de Chantilly, Gavin Wade,
Verity Yeates and the cast and crew who used
other people's cameras and can therefore not
be identified by name.

The film *Feature* was presented in the following exhibitions:

Exhibition Tour Producer: Catherine Williams

FEATURE: ARCHAEOLOGY
            20 June – 12 July 2008
            Leeds Met Gallery
            Leeds Metropolitan University,
            Civic Quarter
            Leeds LS1 3HE
            Curator: Moira Innes

FEATURE: IMAGE
            8 August – 21 September 2008
            Castlefield Gallery
            2 Hewitt Street, Knott Mill,
            Manchester M15 4GB
            Director: Kwong Lee

FEATURE: ARCHITECTURE
            November/December 2008
            Eastside Projects
            86 Heath Mill Lane
            Birmingham B9 4AR
            Curator: Gavin Wade
            Architect/Curator: Celine Condorelli

*Feature* was originally commissioned by Donna Lynas at Wysing Arts Centre, Bourn, with funding from Arts Council England East and Wysing Arts Centre. The film was realised with completion funding from Arts Council England London and the support of Film London Artists' Moving Image Network and further support from the Arts and Humanities Research Council. The *Feature* exhibitions were supported by the National Lottery, through Arts Council England.

A grateful thank you to Donna Lynas, who showed faith in my madness when anyone else would have given up for dead. To Tim Sidell, whose patience and understanding gave the madness form, and to all the artists and volunteers who made the project their own.
            Shezad Dawood, May 2008

CASTLEFIELD GALLERY

UNIVERSITY OF WESTMINSTER

BOO KWO RKS

# TRAILER

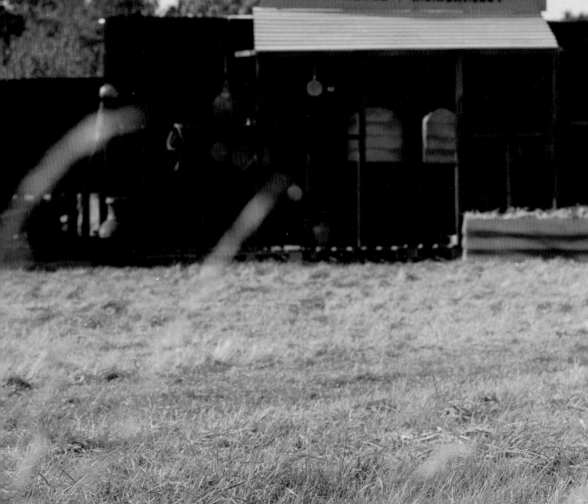

WHEN SHEZ FIRST ASKED ME TO PLAY THE SHERIFF IN HIS WESTERN I THOUGHT HE WAS NUTS!

SHEZ, WHAT THE HELL DO I KNOW ABOUT BEING A SHERIFF!?! I'M FROM QUEENS, FOR CHRIST'S SAKE! GET RICHARD PRINCE. THAT'S MORE HIS KIND OF THING.

DOUGIE, *BABY!!!* YOU WERE BORN TO PLAY THIS PART!!! PRINCE CAN'T ACT TO SAVE HIS LIFE. AND BESIDES, HE'S TOO DRUNK TO STAND UP HALF THE TIME!!!

JUST PLAY IT LIKE SLY IN COPLAND. HAS ANYONE EVER TOLD YOU YOU LOOK *JUST* LIKE HIM !

YOU KNOW THE LAST TIME I HEARD *THAT* COMPARISON I WAS IN A STRIP CLUB, SO I'M NOT SURE I BUY IT...

YOU EVEN GET TO BE EATEN BY *ZOMBIES!!!*

I BET YOU HEAR THIS *ALL* THE TIME, BUT...

TO BE HONEST, I ALWAYS SAW MYSELF AS MORE OF A *WHITE* DENZEL WASHINGTON...

MY MAN!!!

BUT MAYBE I *DO* LOOK LIKE STALLONE A LITTLE...KIND OF A *POOR MAN'S* VERSION...

SERIOUSLY, YOU COULD *TOTALLY* BE HIS COUSIN!!!

SO I FIGURED WHAT THE HECK!

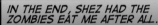